I0200687

Paperback Quarterly

*"Journal of the
American Paperback Institute"*

CONTENTS

The Pecan Valley Press
Brownwood, Texas

Paperback Quarterly is published by the American Paperback Institute. The goal of API is to make the history of mass-market paperbacks, their publishers, authors, illustrators, and distributors more comprehensive and reliable.

Paperback Quarterly features articles and notes dealing with every type (mystery, detective, science fiction, western, adventure, etc) and with every aspect of new, old and rare paperbacks.

Emphasis is placed on the historical research of paperbacks, their authors, illustrators, publishers and distributors; but the editors also invite contributions of bibliographical interest. In short, the only criterion for the editors' consideration is that the subject matter pertain to paperbacks.

Paperback Quarterly pays 1 cent per word (200-4,000 words) for articles and notes. Payment on acceptance.

Paperback Quarterly is published in Spring, Summer, Fall and Winter of each year with a subscription rate of $6.00 per year or individual copies for $2.00 each. Institutional and library subscriptions are $8.00 per year. Overseas rate is $12.00. All back issues are currently out of print.

All correspondence, articles, notes, queries, ads and subscriptions should be sent to 1710 Vincent St., Brownwood, Texas 76801. (915) 643-1182.

Published and Edited by

Charlotte Laughlin   Billy C. Lee

Contributing Editors

Bill Crider   Thomas Bonn

Printer and Technical Advisor
Martin E. Gottschalk

Cover Logo Designer
Peter Manesis

Letters

Over the last several months, Barry Pattengill and William J. Denholm III have written PQ several letters adding to Jim Sanderson's listing of Flagship books in the Fall, 1979 issue. The following additional list of Flagship books is a composite of their letters.

THE CLONES by P.T. Olemy (092-00840-060, 1968, 60¢, "A Flagship Science Fiction Tale")

LOVE SPY, LOVE by Roy Charles Kasper (092-00843-060, 1968, 60¢, "A Flagship Spy Thriller")

MOONSPIN by Elmer J. Carpenter (092-00715-060, 1967, 60¢)

EXILE AND OTHER TALES OF FANTASY by M.A. Cummings (092-00864-060, 1968, 60¢)

PINK DOLPHIN by P.T. Olemy (702, 1967, 60¢)

IN PRAISE OF LOVE by Cole Freedman (092-00714-075, 1967)

In addition, Pattengill writes:

Enjoyed Bill Crider's article in the Fall issue on "Backwoods" novels. A possible addition to the titles Mr. Crider listed is SATAN'S MATE by George H. Smith (Newsstand Library, 1960). This is a "Bayou Country" novel featuring a swamp scene on the cover with two "swamp babes" in a flat-bottom boat being lead by a wading rustic male.

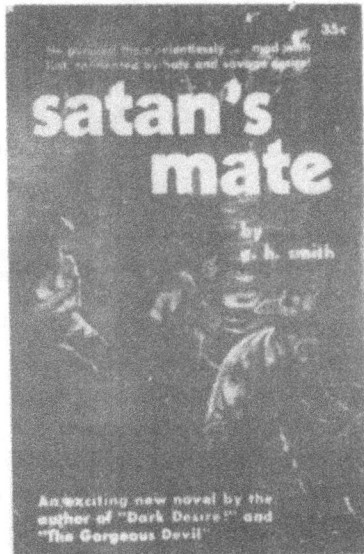

*Frank Halpern and Jan Landau both wrote concerning
the Superior Reprint's A SAKI SAMPLER query by
James Tinsman in the Fall issue.*

Dear Billy,
    I can answer the question raised in James
Tinsman's note concerning Superior Reprints.
Superior Reprint M656 A SAKI SAMPLER by H.H. Munro
was evidently one of the books brought to Bantam
from Superior Reprints by Ian Ballantine. Bantam
added a full-color dust jacket with the title THE
SHE-WOLF AND OTHER STORIES (A SAKI SAMPLER) and its
own serial number 143 at the head of the spine and
at the top left corner of the front cover.
                            Best,
                            Frank Halpern

Dear Billy,
    ...One last point about the SHE-WOLF. The
Bantam dust-wrapper bears #143 on the spine, as
well as in the upper left corner..but no logo nor
name appears on the outer covers. ''Bantam'' appears
only inside the back flap of the d/w. Glad to
help..old paperbacks are a passion..
                            Best regards,
                            Jan Landau

Paperback Quarterly
    I'm enclosing another year's subscription to
PQ, and my thanx for a year's delight and enlighten-
ment. Special thanx for the Winter '79 issue,
especially the article on Bonibooks by Peter
Manesis (I thought the few I'd found were fine--
now I know the best is yet to be found), and Mark
Schaffer on Covers and Culture. I was a little
surprised he didn't mention the Pocket Library, with
its very subdued and distinctive format: the sober
colors and pastels, the often elegant design, the
matt finish, the curious choice of authors and titles..
If anyone there knows something about the
Pocket Library, and thinks they're worth an article,

4

I'd appreciate it. I'd also appreciate some help
with two questions: (1) Could you supply titles
for PL 25, 35, 521, 523, 524? (2) Were PL 1-4 ever
issued as a slipcased set? The hardback edition
was; I'm wondering if the paperback followed suit.
If any of your readers collect the series, I'd
like to hear from them.
Sincerely,
Lloyd Busch

*Pocket Library #25 is TESS OF THE D'URBERVILLES.
I'm not sure the others exist though R. Reginald's
CUMULATIVE PAPERBACK INDEX indicates they do.*

Dear Billy,
     Some Rex Stout collectors will note the ''squid''
error on page 15 of my article; I meant to type
''squib,'' which would also have been wrong. It
should actually read ''squab,'' which Nero Wolfe and
others were using with nine dishes of <u>sauce
printemps</u>. Mea culpa.
     Bill Crider's feature on ''Paperback Bodies''
was a delight. Dell's GIVE 'EM THE AX was first
printed as #389, then reprinted with the same cover
as #460. The cover does not show ''an early version
of the miniskirt,'' as Bill Crider notes; page 59
of the book explains that the girl Billy Prue has
found the corpse in her bathtub just as she was
getting ready to take a bath; ''I flung on the first
thing I could find to cover me up''--i.e., the fur
coat. Of course that doesn't explain why she still
has nylons on, or shoes, but who can say in what
order Miss Billy sheds her all?
Best,
Bill Lyles

Dear Mr. Lee,
     I've only recently heard of your fine magazine.
I've been a collector of pulps for ten years. Last
year I became interested in collecting paperbacks
which were written by former pulp writers. As you
can guess I soon became hooked. I borrowed your

5

back issues from Chuck Miller. I was very impressed by your zine, needless to say, I'm enclosing a check for a years subscription. I'm especially interested in pulp/paperback crossovers.

I really enjoy the color photos you insert in the issues. The cover Chet Williamson mentions that was in the Avon Murder Mystery Monthly article ["*Mighty, Miraculous Murder Mystery Monthly,*" by *Howard Waterhouse, page 31, Volume I, Number 4*] (SHIP OF ISHTAR) was done by Paul Stahr who did very many covers for Argosy during the 1930's. Does anyone know who did those great covers for the Dell Mapbacks; the ones I'm referring to are the symbolic ones.

Best,

J. Barry Traylor

Dear Editors:

In response to Eric Tucker's letter on my omission of Penguin Books from my article, two points are worth mentioning-- 1) My original article was specifically focussed on American paperback cover art, and I felt that the logical place to begin was with De Graff. 2) Viewed within a larger Western framework, Penguin does predate Pocket Books by several years. However, Penguin still seems more of a continuation of a long and relatively neglected tradition of inexpensive reprintings of fiction and non-fiction, while De Graff, if only for his emphasis on visuals, suggested something relatively innovative. Be that as it may, that long tradition of cheap mass literature may spur some interested readers of PQ to explore its history. Then, perhaps, we can better understand why Penguin and Pocket books had the impact they did.

Mark Schaffer

Paperback Writers
by Bill Crider

It's impossible to know where to begin a discussion of Michael Avallone. Is there anything the man hasn't written? He's done one of the longest-running paperback private-eye series. He's done movies into books. He's done television shows into books. He's written for a soft-core porn house. He's done horror. He's written gothics under several names. He wrote the first six books in Award's Nick Carter series. He's now writing Pinnacle's Butcher series. I've probably left out nine or ten things.

Let's start with Ed Noon. Noon began as a hardcover detective with Henry Holt in 1953. You have only to open the book to the wonderfully quirky Cast of Characters--"according to their heights" to know that this isn't going to be the usual private eye novel. Other Noon novels have casts "according to their weapons" or "according to their theme songs" or what have you. All of them that I've read are tough and funny in Avallone's inimitable, whacked-out way, and Noon went on from his first glorious appearance to work for Gold Medal, Belmont, Signet, and Curtis. I haven't seen him around lately, but I hope he'll be back. I sort of miss him.

I don't read gothics, myself, but I'll never forget the charge I got when I first saw one on the stands by "Edwina Noon." What a great

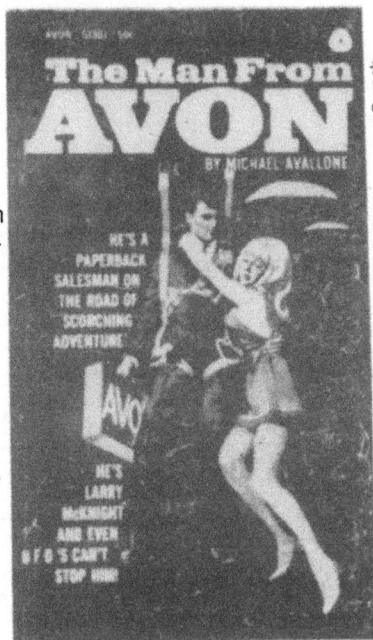

pseudonym! What a great inside joke!

I've only read two of Avallone's Midwood books, SEX KITTEN and SINNERS IN WHITE. Believe me, they have plenty of sex in them, sex that in the early sixties would have been pretty hot stuff, though not nearly so graphic as what's on the stands these days. Sex aside, however, both these novels contain the patented Avallone storytelling. It may be that no one will ever claim that he writes great Literature, but he sure writes great stories.

Avallone even writes for kids. He's done novels based on television's PARTRIDGE FAMILY, and for Scholastic he did CB LOGBOOK OF THE WHITE KNIGHT. If your kid comes home from fourth grade with a brochure from the Arrow Book Club, and it lists the latter title, let the kid order it. I can assure you, it's not a thing like SEX KITTEN.

Recommended titles? Anything about Ed Noon. But I'd also like to recommend THE MAN FROM AVON

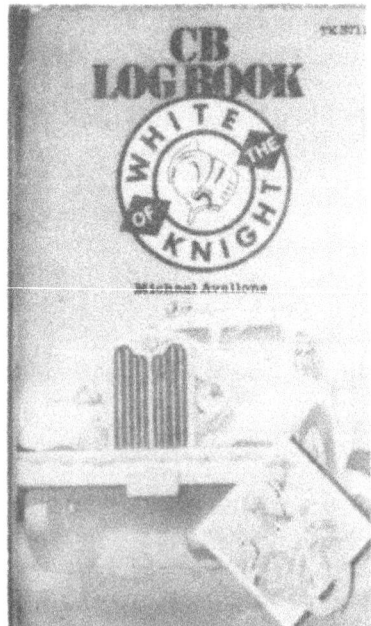

8

(Avon, 1967), in which the hero is a salesman for Avon Books -- and also an undercover government investigator of UFOs. (I'm not kidding; only Avallone could pull this off.) And there's also TALES OF THE FRIGHTENED (Belmont, 1963), twenty six short-short horror tales which were also available on Mercury Records, narrated by Boris Karloff. I suspect that the most collectible Avallone of all would be the Ed Noon novels published in the magazine format, which Avallone mentions in the accompanying interview: Ed NOON AND THE BOUNCING BETTY, ED NOON AND THE ALARMING CLOCK. Much to my regret, I've never seen copies of these books. But that's what collecting's all about. Someday.... Somewhere.....

★ ★ Book dealers ★ ★

Interview with Michael Avallone
by Michael S. Barson

MB: Mike, in front of us we have this rather un-usual publication, "Ed Noon and the Bouncing Betty" -- it was published in a magazine format...Why wasn't this a paperback original or, for that matter, a hardcover?

MA: *We're going back, Mike, to the dear ages of the late '50's...Spillane had had such a tremendous impact on the field--Four years before this date I had picked up a walloping $10,000 reprint price from Henry Holt for the paperback rights to THE TALL DOLORES, and that $10,000 was entirely due to Mr. Spillane, because everyone was searching around for another Mickey Spillane. And here was this little boy from the Bronx with a book that sounded like it was the goods, and Holt felt, boy, we can go to town with this guy, which they did. But then, in the late '50's, the bloom had worn off the Spillane rose. Everybody had cleaned up, Mickey had done about eight Mike Hammers, and the field was flooded with imitations -- Mike Roscoe, hundreds of guys; even the Gold Medal stable had a couple of boys trying to do the same thing -- Curt Cannon, which is a penname for a very famous writer [Evan Hunter] -- so after five fast sales in the private detective field I had to go begging with two or three very, very good novels. After VIOLENCE IN VELVET [1956] there was THE BOUNCING BETTY, THE CRAZY MIXED-UP CORPSE, and THE ALARMING CLOCK.*

MB: Did you tell me earlier that there was an American News strike that was involved with this being a magazine?

MA: *In the summer of '56 I ran into Mr. Lyle Kenyon Engel, now famous, or infamous, for the million* dollars he made for John Jakes on the Bicentennial series. It was a time we were both coming up and growing; he had a great head for publishing ,and he loved Ed Noon. He had encountered a Texas millionaire who had a lot of money to invest in radio packaging and magazines, and he fronted the whole bill for this series of magazines that Lyle and I put out together -- I as editor and Lyle as the brain, and it was Lyle's bright idea to turn out these unsold Ed Noon novels which the market didn't want. Like I said, it was a fallow period. So he had this bright idea: Why not give them a $2.75 novel for 35¢? The original idea was to call it the Ed Noon Mystery Magazine, and I nixed that -- I told Lyle that was too specific a field. So he invented the idea of calling it "Ed Noon and the _____"...("Ed Noon and the Bouncing Betty," "Ed Noon and the Alarming Clock.") The magazine was called basically PRIVATE INVESTIGATOR. It ran for two issues. We did Space Science Fiction, Tales of the Frightened, American Agent --for which Mr. Jakes did the very first novel, called OPERATION ZERO, a beautiful Bond-type novel, one of John's best, which I edited. We didn't give him enough money for it, but that's neither here nor there; he later resold it as a Nick Carter novel for a miserable 500 bucks. Of course, now he's got millions.

But the American News strike came along at just this time, and

Michael Avallone

11

for anybody who doesn't know what that is, you can't really sell a magazine or a book without a distributor; if you haven't got a distributor, you're dead. You could have a hundred thousand copies of the best book in the world, but if you can't get it out to your readers, where the hell are you? Now we're getting into trucks, unions, space on the stands, etc., etc. We had a 75% sale, great fan mail, but we had to fold up the whole operation. It's show business, a writer's life. There are trends.

MB: In front of us we have a stack of Ed Noon classics, and almost every one is with a different house, starting with the 1950s and going into the 1960s. We have a New American Library, a Belmont, a Perma Star--what were the realities of the paperback industry so that a single, consistent character would end up under so many imprints?

MA: *I think the same answer would be valid today. They were interested in quick millions; they wanted a runaway bestseller. Each and every company gave you a shabby $1500 or $2000 advance, which is 4% of the 25¢ cover price, which comes to a penny. Now, it costs them $7000 to print their whole volume. Are you going to try to tell me that selling 200,000 copies at 25¢ a copy-- even with the middle man, they never lose money? But they try you for two or three titles. At Gold*

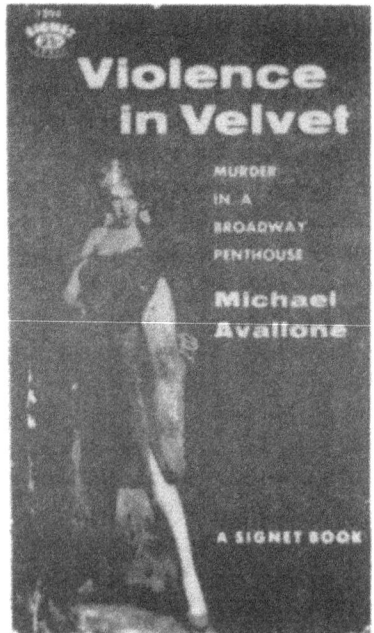

12

Medal, for instance, we did CRAZY MIXED-UP CORPSE, VOODOO MURDERS, MEANWHILE BACK AT THE MORGUE. You could sell 75% of a 200,000 print order--that's not bad--but obviously it's not enough for them.

With the failure of the three Mickey Spillane movies at the box-office, who was Ed Noon? Who was Lew Archer? No one could have cared less. We were miles away from a Paul Newman reviving the thing ten years later with a brilliantly made movie (HARPER). It's a matter of trends. Even as we sit here now, people say to me, "Who needs a private detective?" But we'll be reading them twenty years from now.

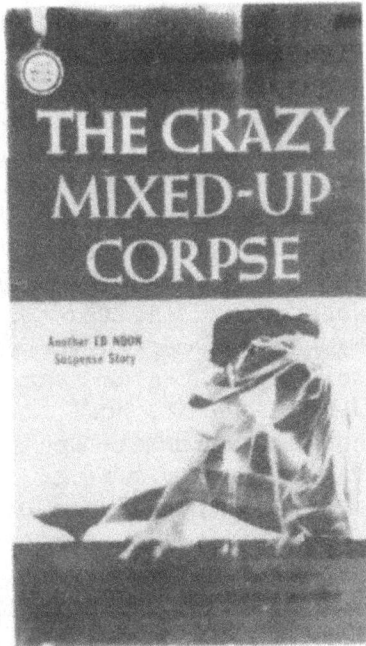

MB: That brings up an interesting point. You were talking about trends--In the early '60s the James Bond thing hit, and the paperback sales went into the millions. That was what was hot in the industry. But James Bond is no an American type of hero. And the spy novel originally was a British sort of thing. Nevertheless, Ed Noon becomes a private investigator/secret agent working for the president. How do you maintain the American individualism of Ed Noon in this type of story?

MA: It's all in the approach. Fleming arrived on our cultural scene because our president (JFK) read him, and PLAYBOY started printing him. I stay American because I'm Michael Avallone and even if I assume a guise, it's still going to come out with that Manhattan/World War II/Hollywood-oriented

13

thing. I cover this all in SHOOT IT AGAIN, SAM, which shows how a thoroughly Hollywood-drenched person will react to a crime--Ed Noon. You cannot hide your orientation, your viewpoint.

I've done several things with the series that no one's ever noticed, and it's always horrified me. I once crossed the private detective novel with the western: THE BRUTAL KOOP. I once pitted Ed Noon against a Mike Hammer type: the Devlin of THERE IS SOMETHING ABOUT A DAME (Belmont, 1963); nobody ever spotted it. It was 1963 and I was sick of being compared to Mickey Spillane when Ed Noon and Hammer are as apart as the poles, like Dr. Jekyll and Mr. Hyde, and here was Ed Noon going up against a Hammer-type in the character of this Vince Devlin, a rival private eye. No critic ever noticed it, including Mr. Boucher. I put a black woman in as his secretary in 1963, and no one ever noticed it. Your reach always exceeds your grasp, but I have tried and dared everything with the Noon novels.

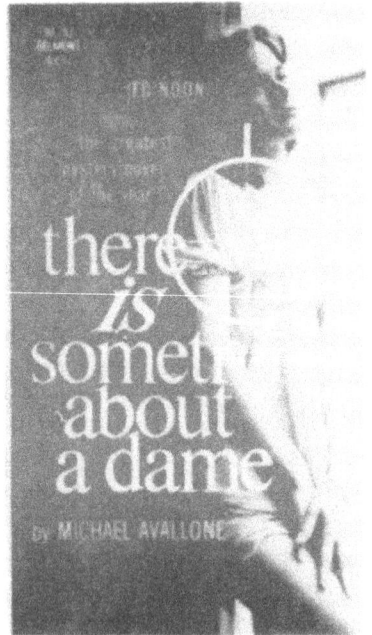

MB: Ed Noon and the private detective novel is just one of so many genres you've worked in--some of them under your own name, some of them not. Which genres do you enjoy working in, and which do you not like? And do you have any problems changing the Avallone writing style to adapt to the gothics, the novelizations (of television shows and films) and so forth?

MA: I have to make a sweeping statement here: I have never written anything I don't like. I would rather write an Ed Noon novel than anything else because that's me; I'm not keeping a daily diary, but he went to the same high school, same love affairs; the only thing I didn't do is make him Italian. But, let me put it this way; I wrote the Midwood titles 'way back in the early '60s when it was considered denigrating to write sex novels. I knew I would have no control over the covers; but I would go to the grave with those books, because in spite of those lurid covers and title changes, those are all very serious novels about their time and place. SEX KITTEN (Midwood #189, 196) was originally titled THE GIRL FROM AVENUE J, which honestly tried to show you, with a little sexual excitement, of course, what would happen to a young kid who ran away from Brooklyn and had a wild weekend in New York. It's strictly on the side of the angels; in fact, I used to have fights with the Midwood editors because I did a book about a call girl, and to make it ultra-realistic I had her have her period. They said, "These guys out there don't want to read about that." But I said, "Look, we're writing about people, even in the framework of entertainment.
     In spite of the fifteen pen names, I've signed my name to everything.

MB: What's the process whereby you are approached for a project like THE MAN FROM UNCLE or HAWAII 5-0 or THE PARTRIDGE FAMILY or BENEATH THE PLANET OF THE APES? How does a writer get such an assignment?

15

MA: It's simpler than it sounds. Let's say you're doing a series for Popular Library; you've written books for them; they know you're a professional-- it doesn't hurt that they know you're a great show business buff, that you love movies. This was the era when they began to realize that money could be made with the tie-in book. (It's more today, of course, with STAR WARS and STAR TREK). They pay a license to CBS. They say, "HAWAII 5-0 is coming up and it looks like a good detective series; we will have Mike Avallone go down and see the pilot; Mike's a good detective story writer." They put you into a screening room, and they roll the picture just for you. Then you report back to whomever sent you, and he says, "Well, what'd you think of it? Is there a book series in it?" I said, "Yeah, it's a great show. Just send me a rap sheet on it. So you go back and do your original novel, and they give you $2000 or $2500 for it...

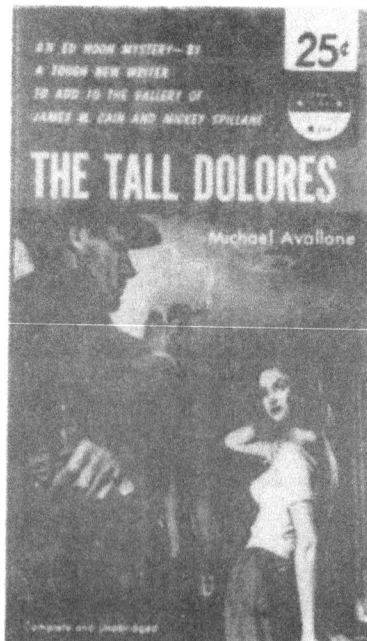

MB: How long do you
spend on a novelization,
since, as you've said,
it's a decent fee but not
a large one?

MA: If a man can write a
completely original 60,000
word to 75,000-word novel
in four days, five days,
six days, doesn't it
stand to reason if he has
a thoroughly developed
script in front of him
that he could knock it
out in two or three days?
I did one in a day and
a half; it was a rush
job.

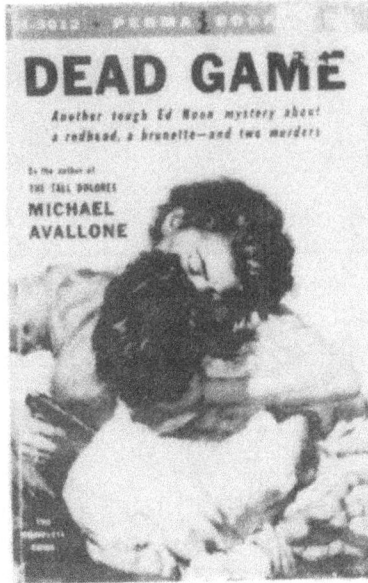

DEAD GAME

Another tough Ed Noon mystery about
a redhead, a brunette—and two murders

THE TALL DOLORES
MICHAEL
AVALLONE

James Meese

MB: There are some different kinds of problems when
you inherit a series, such as THE BUTCHER, where--
no matter who originally created it--it has now become a property that the publisher wants to keep
intact for the fans that buy it number by number by
number. What kinds of problems are there in being
consistent within the restrictions of this character
on whom somebody has already done 25 books?

MA: You made a very good point. Andy Ettinger,
when they decided to revive the Butcher series,
which they had made a lot of money on through 26
titles, wanted to do a package of three, but he
wanted my ideas on it. He gave me a lot of the
books to read, and I read them, and I came back and
said,"This is comic book stuff; it's super-silly,
lots of action, lots of violence, minimum of charac-
terization, guns, girls." I said, "I'd love to do
this series, even though it's going to be under a
house pen name, but I'd like to make him a little
more human, a little more vulnerable--'cause this

17

guy knocks off about fifteen people a book, and that's a bit much."

MB: That would take care of Ed Noon for the rest of his career!

MA: Having to work on the proviso that I wanted to make him more human, but he still had to be the gutsy Butcher, I dedicated the book to Mickey Spillane and I, THE JURY. It's Ed Noon motivated with a sense of vengeance.

MB: I can see how a guy like Michael Avallone can make the transition from the private eye to another action character, even if he is psychotic like the Butcher. But you said you had also written gothics and romances. That can't be easy for a writer whose forte is action. What are the problems involved in doing that kind of work?

MA: That is an effort, because I like to work fast and to be succinct. But part of you reacts to the challenge, and I'd rather write than eat. Now, in a gothic you have to hang the drapes. The four basic rules of the gothic: damsel in distress; old, dark house; the old vs. the new; and atmosphere. In the gothic, you do have to spend longer describing the furniture, the milieu. But by the time I had come to this, I was ready for it. I wouldn't have liked it when I was 25, but at 38 or 40, I was ready to go a little slower, take a little longer. I enjoy setting the eerie mood.

[Mike Barson is currently working on his PhD in American Culture at Bowling Green State University.]

● ● WANTED ● ●

Back issues of **PAPERBACK QUARTERLY** Volume I through Volume II, Number 3. Olle Bolming, Katarina Bangata 56, 116 39 Stockholm, SWEDEN.

Recent Releases

COLLECTIBLE BOOKS: SOME NEW PATHS. Jean
Peters, editor (R.R. Bowker, 1979) 294 pp.

This delightful new book fulfills its prefa-
tory promise of doing for the 1980s what John
Carter's classic NEW PATHS IN BOOK COLLECTING did
in the 1930s. As John Carter later wrote about
book collecting, "...the man of enterprise will
want to strike out some new line, or give a new
twist to a familiar one."

COLLECTIBLE BOOKS contains nine chapters point-
ing out new lines and new twists to that most convi-
vial of arts--book collecting. In my experience in
the field, I have found fellow collectors to be a-
mong the most interesting, intelligent, and gracious
persons of my acquaintance; and this book bears out
my observation.

William B. Todd, who wrote the third chapter,
"Books in Series," served on my doctoral committee
at the University of Texas and taught me courses in
bibliography, which were as entertaining as they
were informative. He introduced me to Thomas J.
Wise and to those great literary detectives, John
Carter and Graham Pollard; to the ABC'S OF BOOK
COLLECTING and to the agfa lupe; and with a gracious
humor he taught me that serif was not spelled the
same as "seraph." (At that time, you see, my
experience with angels was much wider than my experience with bibliography.)

His chapter on series books is as interesting,
entertaining, and informative as were his classes.
Of special interest to the readers of PQ is the
eight-page section on the Tauchnitz series--a great,
great grandfather of mass-market paperbacks. You
will also be interested in his references to Hans

Schmoller's "The Paperback Revolution," in ESSAYS
IN THE HISTORY OF PUBLISHING, edited by Asa Briggs,
and to David J. Hall's "The Penguin Collectors'
Story," in ANTIQUARIAN BOOK MONTHLY REVIEW 5 (September 1978). You may not find those references on
a first reading of the chapter, but Bill Todd also
taught me that the most interesting part of any
book or essay was always in the footnotes. So
read those notes!

G. Thomas Tanselle wrote the first chapter, in
which he advocates the collecting of "Non-firsts."
I met him once or twice when he was in Austin using
the rare book collections of the Humanities Research
Center. At a small party given in his honor in the
home of Warner Barnes (another eminent bibliographer
and collector), Tanselle mused that Warner might
take all the mystery out of bibliography with his
use of Ph-meters, Beta radiography, and "chemistry";
but he urbanely concluded that such a feat would
require alchemy and not chemistry. The impression
of his intelligence which I received in our brief
conversations has been confirmed by his intelligent
decision to subscribe to PQ.

Everything Tanselle writes about the importance
of non-firsts in publication history applies to
paperback reprints, a field which has previously
been scorned by such collectors of paperback originals as PQ's own Bill Crider. Parts of Tanselle's
essay are quoted in Billy Lee's article, "Reprints/
Reprints" in this issue of PQ, but you will want to
read the entire essay for its erudite consideration
of non-firsts.

Thomas L. Bonn, a contributing editor of PQ
has written the fifth chapter of COLLECTIBLE BOOKS,
entitled (what else?) "American Mass-Market Paperbacks." I regret that we have never met, but our
correspondence has been interesting and profitable.
His annotated bibliography, "Mass-Market Paperback
Publishing, 1939-Present," found in PQ, Vol. 1, no.4,
has become an indispensable tool to the editors of
PQ and to many other collectors as well.

His 34-page chapter in COLLECTIBLE BOOKS includes photographs of fifteen paperback book covers and a page of animal logos. It gives a working definition of "mass-market," provides a history of early paperback publishing (basically 1939-1952), and makes suggestions for possible directions to adopt in creating an interesting paperback collection.

He warns the new collector against the temptation to collect "everything" instead of clearly defining the scope of the paperback collection, whether it be "Agatha Christie softcover who-dunits, first paperback editions of Lion Books, animal logos, Bantam endpaper maps of Rafael Palocios, the cover art of Harry Bennet, or any of the other endless possibilities in the paperback field."

I must confess that I tend to amass as much as I select, and I find a certain greedy pleasure in amassing books. Once when my greedy pleasure in books was evident in Larry McMurtry's bookshop in Georgetown, he assured me that in time my "passion for books would give way to knowledge." I didn't know that he was the Larry McMurtry (and he certainly didn't know that I was the Charlotte Laughlin); I just knew that I was in the best bookshop I had yet found in Washington, D.C., and that I had expected a proprietor who came in drinking a Dr. Pepper to be a little more friendly and a little less superior in tone. I irately replied that I would prefer passion to knowledge any day.

One of the delights of COLLECTIBLE BOOKS is that it has done much to increase my knowledge without noticeably abating my passion. Now that's a good book for you!

In addition to the chapters already mentioned, the book contains seven more essays by collectors: "A Backward Look: The Sadleir Circle in Perspective"; "American Trade Bindings and Their Designers, 1880-1915"; "Film Books"; "Photography as Book Illustration, 1839-1900"; "Book Catalogues"; and "Publishers' Imprints." The final chapter, "American Fiction since 1960," is by Peter B. Howard, an antiquarian bookdealer. Since so many important contemporary works of fiction have appeared in paperback in the last two decades, Howard devotes space to the discussion of paperbacks. "Try to find a Regency or Lion or Brandon House or Essex House paperback original!" he challenges. In this chapter Howard includes photographs of two Regency originals: WEED (1961) and BLACK! (1963) by the black author, Clarence L. Cooper, Jr. This chapter is another one that will be of particular interest to readers of PQ.

A book that increases both passion and knowledge in book collecting is well worth the $16.95 investment. You may order it from the R.R. Bowker Order Department; P.O. Box 1807; Ann Arbor, Michigan 48106.

------Charlotte Laughlin

★ ★

Chloe's Books

P.O. Box 255673
Sacramento, CA 95825

We would like to purchase the following paperbacks:

Atlle, Phillip.   THE IRSH BEAUTY CONTRACT (Gold Medal)
Chandler, Raymond.
    THE BIG SLEEP.(New Avon Library #38)
    FIVE SINISTER CHARACTERS (New Avon Library #88)
    LITTLE SISTER (Pocket Book #750)
Leigh, Michael. VELVET UNDERGROUND, 1st printing
    (MacFadden Books)
MacDonald, John Ross. MY NAME IS ARCHER, 1st printing 1955
    (Bantam)
TWO LANE BLACKTOP (Award Books)
Avon Murder Mystery Monthlies: numbers 7,19,28,43.

Alfred Hitchcock: Dell Paperbacks
by Billy C. Lee and Charlotte Laughlin

"Du-du-dudududum-de-dum...Good Eev-ening..."
I can nearly hear Hitchock's slow, monotone
come alive. That familiar beginning from his TV
days has indeed become a classic. It's safe to say
that everyone is familiar with Hitchcock's film
(both TV and movie) accomplishments. His movie pro-
ductions span more than half a century with such
films as "Sabatoge"(1936), "The Trouble with Harry"
(1955), "North by Northwest" (1959), "Psycho" (1960),
and "The Birds" (1961).

Readers, as well as movie-goers, are more
familiar with Hitchcock films than with Hitchcock
paperbacks. Alfred Hitchcock does not write stories
anymore than he writes his film scripts. Rather,
according to William Lyles[*], Hitchcock lent his
name to Dell for use on the mapback anthologies of
terror stories, in return for the sum of $1,000 per
book. As Michael Avallone says, "Alfred Hitchcock
never wrote a line in his life. He doesn't have to.
He's one of the greatest directors that ever lived."

Lyles writes that Don[ald G.] Ward edited and
wrote the introductions for several of the early
books. Don Ward, who occasionally used the pseudonym "Tracy Powers," worked as an editor at Western
Publishing Co. in Racine, Wisonsin and in New York,
from 1945-1955. After 1955, he has worked as a
free-lance editor for many publishers, including
Dell.

Another author/editor of Hitchcock books is
Robert Arthur. He packaged a number of hardbacks
for Random House and actually invented the series
about three kids as investigators (ALFRED HITCHCOCK
AND THE THREE INVESTIGATORS: THE SECRET OF TERROR
KID, and others). As Michael Avallone explains,

[William L. (Bill) Lyles is currently working on a history of Dell Books.]

these books, like the paperbacks, were sold under the Hitchcock name in hopes that it would sell books; but Robert Arthur wrote the books. "But the crummy thing about this is that nobody notices the words 'text by Robert Arthur or whomever' except people in the profession," Avallone says. "The same thing has happened to me before, too. For instance, an edition of TALES OF THE FRIGHTENED makes it look like Boris Karloff wrote it, but it says 'text by Avallone'," he added.

The paperbacks give Robert Arthur even less recognition than do the hardbacks. At least four of the Hitchcock paperbacks published by Dell acknowledge the "invaluable assistance of Robert Arthur." These titles are TERROR TIME, DATES WITH DEATH (originally TALES FROM A MONTH OF MYSTERY), STORIES NOT FOR THE NERVOUS, AND TWELVE STORIES FOR LATE AT NIGHT. In addition to editing and "assisting" in the production of Dell paperbacks, Robert Arthur contributed one of his own stories to each of the following Hitchcock anthologies: MORE OF MY FAVORITES IN SUSPENSE, ONCE UPON A DREADFUL

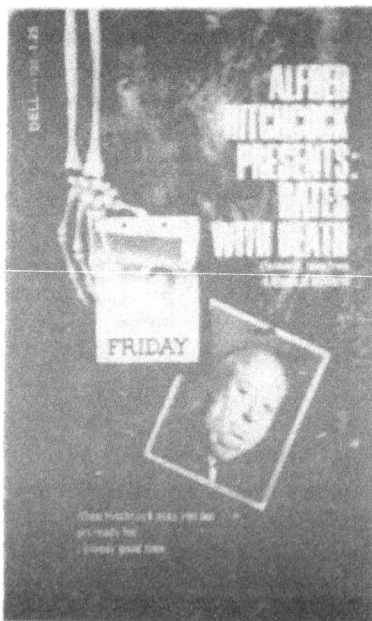

TIME, STORIES MY MOTHER NEVER TOLD ME, SCREAM ALONG WITH ME, A HANG-MAN'S DOZEN, TWELVE STORIES FOR LATE AT NIGHT, and THIRTEEN MORE STORIES THEY WOULDN'T LET ME DO ON TV. Arthur continued work with Hitchcock anthologies until his death in 1969. He's a fine author who has not yet received the recognition he deserves. His accomplishments also include being a radio writer for the "Shadow" series.

Harold Q. Masur is acknowledged for "invaluable assistance" in the production of STORIES TO STAY A-WAKE BY. He has been an associate editor of Alfred Hitchcock anthologies and has contributed stories to TERROR TIME and MURDER-GO-ROUND. Masur has been an author and editor since 1947, when Simon &Schuster published his novel, BURY ME DEEP. In 1957, he edited the paperback original, DOLLS ARE MURDER (Lion Books #152); and in 1962 Pyramid published his novel, THE NAME IS JORDAN, as another paperback original.

A third person acknowledged as giving "valuable assistance" is Patricia O'Connell, for her work on MORE OF MY

FAVORITES IN SUSPENSE, 1964.

But no matter who wrote, selected, and edited the Dell paperbacks, they are all promoted in a style that has become familiar to millions as "Hitchcock."

Paperbacks capitalizing on Hitchcock's name and face began in 1945 with the publication of SUSPENSE (Dell #92). This was the beginning of a long and successful business arrangement between Dell and Hitchcock which continues today. The SUSPENSE cover is a fine example of paperback cover art. The disjointed typography of the word, "suspense," on a white background emphasizes the title. And the drawing of Hitchcock's face, with the effective spider/spiderweb foreground, is superb. In his research William Lyles has found the name of cover artist Lolla MacDonald linked with this cover, but he has not yet established with certainty that she did this painting.

The introduction of SUSPENSE focuses on the definition and quality of suspense, with comments on each of the fourteen stories--a good beginning for the entertaining introductions which were to follow in later years.

The 1964 edition of SUSPENSE, retitled ALFRED HITCHCOCK'S FOURTEEN STORIES TO PLAY RUSSIAN ROULETTE BY (Dell #3632), proclaims on the copyright page to be a new edition of Dell #92. They both contain the same introduction, and thirteen of the fourteen stories are the same. However, the first story featured in Dell #92, "Leinengen Versus the Ants" (which supplied the subject for the mapback), is replaced in this later edition by C.B. Gilford's "Never Kill for Love."

The second Hitchcock mapback, BAR THE DOORS (Dell #143, 1946), contains thirteen "terror" stories. The first printing of BAR THE DOORS certainly features an appropriate cover for terror stories but lacks Hitchcock's picture, which was to become a trademark in later editions. The cover of the next edition of BAR THE DOORS (Dell

Fred Banbery

Earl Sherwan

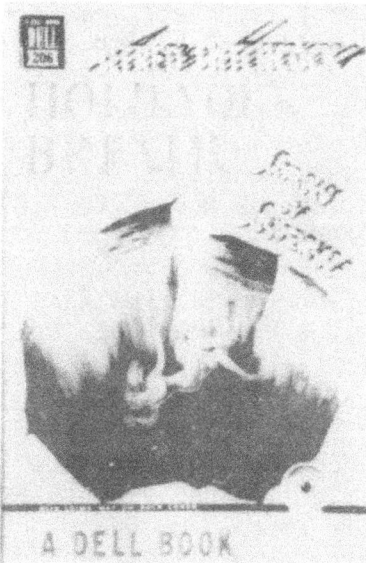

#F166, 1962) does feature Hitchcock, pictured using
a file to break out of jail. And a still later
edition (Dell #0436, 1965) shows an eerie, ghost-
like drawing of Hitchcock with a skeleton hand
opening a door.

The third Hitchcock mapback was HOLD YOUR
BREATH (Dell #206, 1947). This cover, by Earl
Sherman, shows a woman falling into a chasm. But
the cover of a later edition (Dell #3658, 1963)
features Hitchcock holding his own severed head in
a shovel in more distinctive Hitchcock style.

Hitchcock mapbacks continued with ROPE (Dell
#262, 1948) next in line. It certainly has an
effective cover, but not because of a picture of
Hitchcock. Instead of a familiar picture of
Hitchcock, a large black-and-white photo of James
Stewart (against a colorful yellow/green/red background) dominates the cover. This cover successfully attracted movie fans in the late 1940s and
continues to attract collectors of movie editions
today. Unlike the earlier books, ROPE is not a
collection of stories; rather it is an early paperback movie tie-in. For you movie buffs, "Rope" is
Hitchcock's first full-color movie, and the first
Trans-Atlantic Pictures movie. James Stewart was
paid $300,000 for his part in the movie; the entire
film cost 1.5 million--a large expenditure for
1947-48. Later successful Hitchcock movie tie-ins
include PSYCHO, FRENZY, and MARNIE.

FEAR AND TREMBLING (Dell #264, 1948) also
lacks Hitchcock on the cover, but what a replace-
ment! This first edition features a close-up
drawing of a woman's face with her mouth wide open
and with her hair standing on end. This cover
aptly complements the title.

The sixth and last Hitchcock Dell mapback is
also interesting in its own right. SUSPENSE STORIES
(Dell #367, 1950) has the only cover from the
entire Hitchcock line-up featuring a girl with
revealed bosom instead of featuring a bizarre
terror cover as did his earlier and later paper-

28

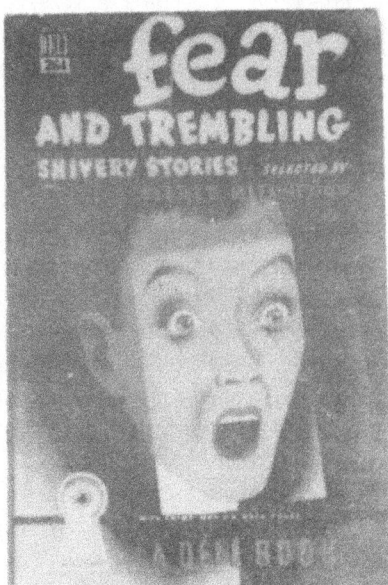

backs. This was the Hitchcock line's only conces-
sion to sexy covers. Afterall, Hitchcock did not
need sex to sell books. The formula of kinky violence without the diversion of sex is a Hitchcock
tradition.

The last story in SUSPENSE STORIES is a western, "Fool's Heart," and is featured on the mapback. It is interesting that Hitchcock has produced
almost every type of film, including a comedy ("The
Trouble with Harry," starring John Forsythe); but he
never produced a western.

It should be noted here that SUSPENSE STORIES
is not a later edition of SUSPENSE (Dell #92, 1945)
as is indicated in THE CUMULATIVE PAPERBACK INDEX
1939-1959 by R. Reginald.

Dell waited eight years to produce another
Hitchcock paperback (ALFRED HITCHCOCK'S TWELVE
STORIES THEY WOULDN'T LET ME DO ON TV; Dell #D231,
1958), and by that time the price had risen to 35¢.
For two reasons, this book is a landmark of Hitchcock paperbacks. With it, Dell begins using his
face on these first editions, repeatedly if not

exclusively. This marketing trend lasted through the early 1970s for a very good reason.

The television programs "Alfred Hitchcock Presents" (1955-1961) and "The Alfred Hitchcock Hour" (1961-1965) made his face and silhouette known to millions of viewers. Of course, Hitchcock had long been making cameo appearances in his movies, starting with "The Lodger" in 1927. And even though the entire movie "Lifeboat" was filmed aboard a lifeboat, Hitchcock managed to get in the picture by having his photo in a newspaper that happened to be on the lifeboat.

TV increased the recognition value of Hitchcock's face, so that it practically became a trademark for the paperbacks. In the 60s and 70s, Hitchcock's face was used on nearly all first editions and reprints of earlier editions to "cash in" on Hitchcock's well-known face.

Beginning with ALFRED HITCHCOCK'S TWELVE STORIES THEY WOULDN'T LET ME DO ON TV, the introductions to Hitchcock paperbacks ceased being true prefaces (which merely introduced the subsequent stories) and became stories in themselves, totally independent of the anthology which followed. They became humorous, witty anecdotes all packed with peculiar insights. But everyone is familiar with Alfred Hitchcock's introductions if he has seen any of his marvelous TV presentations in the 50s and 60s. People know his dry, bizarre wit. His unexpected story twists and endings of his TV stories are no different from his paperback introductions. You can almost hear Hitchcock speaking as you read his introductions. The writers of the paperback introductions had mastered the style made famous by the television programs. The Hitchcock style has become synonymous with the words "bizarre," "weird," "unexpected"; and the paperback introductions do not disappoint us.

In ALFRED HITCHCOCK'S ANTI-SOCIAL REGISTER (Dell #0216, 1965), the introduction gives us a run-down on the customs of Halloween and why

"Hitchcock" is in favor of abolishing the holiday.
He says Halloween has become a "crashing bore"
only surpassed by Father's Day. After a rather
lengthy historical account of Halloween, the introduction relates youthful trick-or-treating days:

> When we rapped on a man's door and hollered,
> 'Trick or Treat!' we expected to be 'treated'
> to nothing less than the contents of his wall
> safe or its equivalent in pastry. Failing
> this, we perpetrated 'tricks'... ...longbows,
> maces, corrosive acids, parangs, bolas, bec-
> ketts, waddies and garrotes were just a few of
> the implements of our vengeance.

This introduction, like so many of them, seems to
become a type of soapbox. And from that crazy,
Hitchcock fashion, the reader can't be sure if it
is serious or not. It is convincing. The "Halloween" introduction concludes:

> But I do think it's vital that we recognize
> a strong tendency in every normal, healthy
> child to be uncivilized. Halloween gives him
> an excellent chance to exercise the antisocial
> attitudes he's contained the rest of the year.

In ALFRED HITCHCOCK'S HAPPINESS IS A WARM
CORPSE (Dell #3438), the introduction takes a
humorous look at human psychology as illustrated
through a story about Hitchcock buying, with delight, what he thinks are stolen suits. He is
sorely disappointed and feels cheated when he finds
out the suit establishment is on the up-and-up.
Be sure to read this one for fun.
Though all of the Hitchcock introductions are
certainly worth reading, some are naturally better
than others. In ALFRED HITCHCOCK'S GAMES KILLERS
PLAY (Dell #2790, 1968), the introductory voice of
Hitchcock speaks briefly about the Academy Award
selections. He believes many of the award-winning

movies have endings which are too "bland" and suggests alternate endings for "Gone with the Wind," "Gigi," and "West Side Story"-- all interestingly Hitchcock.

One of the most humorous Hitchcock introductions is found in COFFIN CORNER (Dell #1323, 1969) (nice photo cover of Hitchcock too). In this anecdote, a famous throat doctor's theory about people saying the word "ah" suggests that Hitchcock might have a career in opera. According to the introduction, Hitchcock begins practicing his singing throughout the day. He learns quickly not to practice in the shower since his booming voice carries further and disturbes the upstairs neighbor (a milkman) who pounds on the floor in anger. Hitchcock hastens to explain the throat doctor's "ah" theory to the milkman who begins practicing too. The singing milkman, however, makes the mistake of singing in the shower and disturbs his upstairs neighbor. The milkman's infuriated upstairs neighbor strikes

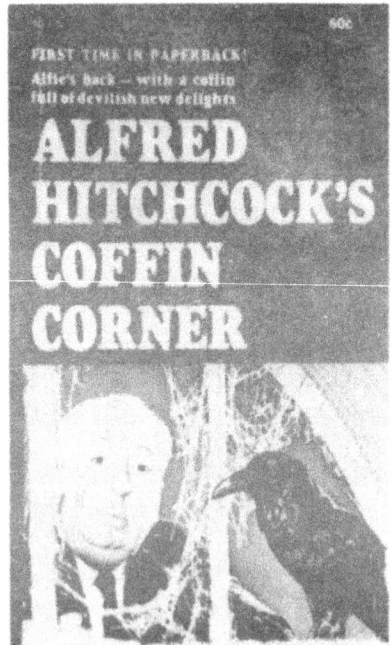

Fred Banbery

his floor with a hammer and dislodges a large hunk of plaster which kills the milkman. A totally absurb, ridiculous story in which someone gets killed, but the telling makes it funny. The opera story ends with a moral: "A word to all aspiring opera singers. Learn from the mistakes of others and don't ever sing while under the shower."

Again, the style of the introduction is just the way millions have heard Hitchcock talk on TV. Such a story easily could have been taken from his TV series.

And like many of the TV stories, ALFRED HITCH- COCK'S NOOSE REPORTS (Dell #6455, 1966) has an introduction that provides us with an example of how bizarre (not in a terrifying or morbid way but rather in a reposterous, unexpected way) Hitchcock- type stories can be. In NOOSE REPORTS, the intro- duction uses a statistical approach to convince us that crime is on the decline. It then paints a sympathetic view of the criminal out of work and

Fred Banbery

33

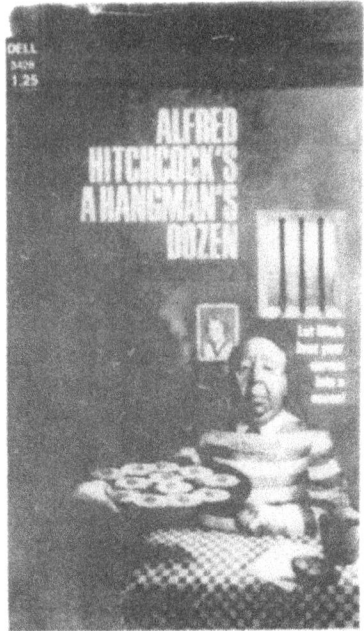

discusses the high overhead cost of the criminal.
This introduction is nearly a "Saturday Night Live"
skit.

As bizarre as the Hitchcock paperback introductions are, the paperback covers are their match.
ALFRED HITCHCOCK'S LET IT ALL BLEED OUT (Dell #4755,
1973) features great graphics. "LET IT" is bright
red, "ALL" is bright pink, "BLEED" is pale pink,
and "OUT" is off-white. The color changes graphic-
ally create the effect that the blood has indeed
all drained away, leaving the last word of the title
as pale as death.

Another great cover is ALFRED HITCHCOCK'S
ONCE UPON A DREADFUL TIME (Dell #6622, 1964). The
severed head effect is skillfully done.

And of interest to cover collectors is ALFRED
HITCHCOCK'S DEATH CAN BE BEAUTIFUL (Dell #1755, 1972)
which features a skeleton in a black cowl pouring
Hitchcock a glass of wine. Hitchcock is lying
comfortably in a hammock which is half by two grave-

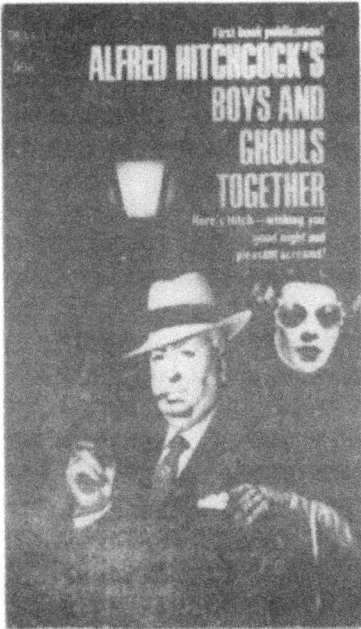

First book publication!
ALFRED HITCHCOCK'S
BOYS AND
GHOULS
TOGETHER
Here's Hitch—wishing you good night and pleasant screams!

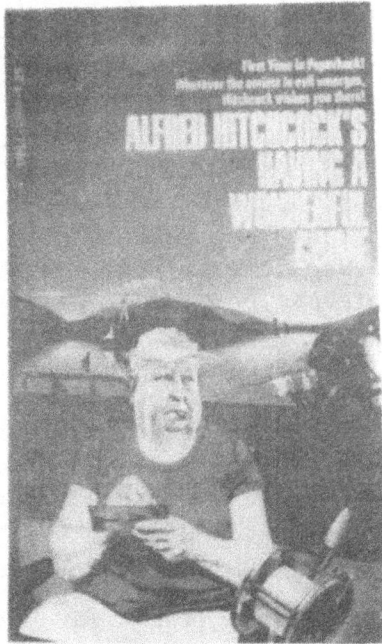

First Time in Paperback!
ALFRED HITCHCOCK'S
HAVING A
WONDERFUL
CRIME

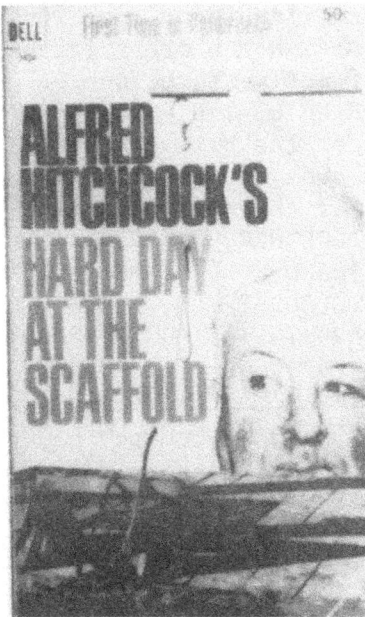

DELL
First Time in Paperback
50¢
ALFRED
HITCHCOCK'S
HARD DAY
AT THE
SCAFFOLD

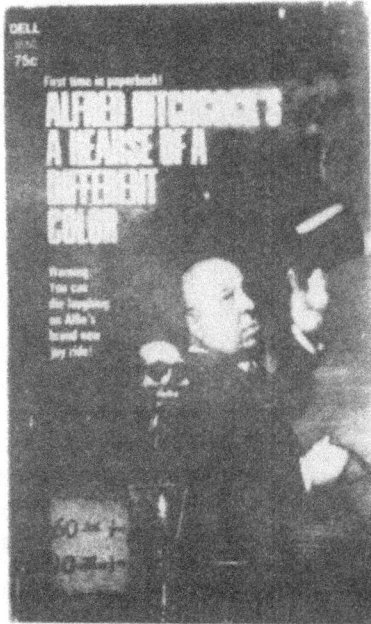

DELL
75¢
First time in paperback!
ALFRED HITCHCOCK'S
A HEARSE OF A
DIFFERENT
COLOR

stones. Hitchcock is reading one of his own books which happens to be the December 1970 edition of ALFRED HITCHCOCK'S SCREAM ALONG WITH ME (Dell #3633).

Perhaps the most interesting cover is ALFRED HITCHCOCK'S A HANGMAN'S DOZEN (Dell #3428, 1976). This $1.25 edition depicts Hitchcock about to eat his last meal before being hanged. He is being served twelve fried eggs by the masked hangman. Interestingly, in real life, Hitchcock detests eggs--ironically appropriate for a Hitchcock cover. Also of interest is the graffiti on the prison walls: A 1940's Kilroy was here, a 1960's peace sign, a game of (what else?) hangman, a tic-tac-toe game, a heart with an arrow through it, and a seemingly out of place portrait of a woman. It would be interesting to know if Hitchcock had any-thing to do with designing his paperback covers. According to John Russell Taylor's biography of Hitchcock, HITCH: THE LIFE & TIMES OF ALFRED HITCHCOCK, Hitchcock did draw his silhouette which has become so famous. An earlier edition of A HANGMAN'S DOZEN (1966) gives us a look at another unusual and effective illustrating technique. On this cover, the artist features Hitchcock's face as part of a building. This effective technique is repeated on MORE STORIES FOR LATE AT NIGHT (1962).

Another characteristic of the Hitchcock books is the use of play-on words puns in the titles. The examples are numerous. Of those not yet men-tioned are BOYS AND GHOULS TOGETHER, HAVING A WONDERFUL CRIME, GET ME TO THE WAKE ON TIME, DEATH ON ARRIVAL, DOWN BY THE OLD BLOODSTREAM, MURDER-GO-ROUND, DON'T LOOK A GIFT SHARK IN THE MOUTH, HARD DAY AT THE SCAFFOLD, and A HEARSE OF A DIFFERENT COLOR.

It's apparent when looking at Hitchcock paper-backs as a whole, Dell has used Hitchcock's face, name, and a bizarre wit coupled with unusual graphics and titles to successfully sell paperbacks.

Reprints/Reprints
by Billy C. Lee

I got the idea for REPRINTS/REPRINTS from G. Thomas
Tanselle's chapter, "Non-Firsts," in COLLECTIBLE
BOOKS: SOME NEW PATHS. (See "New Releases" in this
issue.) Although Tanselle is primarily addressing
19th century hardbacks, his comments apply to the
printing history of mass-market paperbacks.
Tanselle says:

> The activity of a publishing firm cannot be
> represented simply by first.....If one title
> went through 15 printings while another re-
> quired only a single printing, the fact should
> be discoverable from an imprint collection:
> copies of all 15 printings must be there to
> reflect accurately the total output of the firm,
> as well as to suggest the relative popularity
> of the titles it published.
>
> Providing evidence about popularity of course,
> is one of the reasons for the significance
> of non-firsts. ...Obviously one does not have
> the whole story without knowing the number of
> copies in these printings, but such information
> is not always available, and the non-first
> themselves are crucial for whatever facts they
> preserve.

If nothing else, just the physical assembling of
every printing of all of Pocket Books (every
printing) indicates to us the popularity of each
of the books published, and at least an inkling of
the relative number of copies printed. This means
that each of the 80 printings of LOST HORIZON which
now exist is important in understanding the complete
history of the publisher, Pocket Books. Everyone
who has been collecting only first printings of
Ellergy Queen, Agatha Christie, or Rex Stout had
better think twice. I hear from Bill Lyles that
Anna Prentice is collecting every printing of Earl
Stanley Gardner books--now that's a collector with
ambition!

"Lost Horizon"

When LOST HORIZON was first published in hardback in 1933, it did not sell very well. That same year, however, Hilton's GOOD-BYE MR. CHIPS became a best-seller. In the wake of the latter book's success, LOST HORIZON was soon rediscovered and also became a best-seller. In 1937 the first movie of LOST HORIZON was made, and two short years later, Robert De Graff began it all by choosing LOST HORIZON to be Pocket Book number 1. The first Pocket Book printing was in May 1939; and a 5th printing was necessary by the following September. By the end of 1940, LOST HORIZON had seen 11 printings, and by the end of 1942, 21 printings.

Through the 34th printing (July 1945) Pocket Books maintained the original Steinberg cover done in muted shades of blue and purple. The now famous Gertrude, reading a book through spectacles, was conspicuously featured in the lower right-hand corner of the book. I haven't seen the covers of the 35th through the 42nd printings, and I'm not sure what cover was used by Pocket Books. Can anyone narrow the gap?

But the 43rd printing (September 1959) has an entirely different cover, featuring a sleeker Gertrude without spectacles in the upper left-hand corner. This Tom Dunn cover shows a man in military uniform and an oriental woman dressed in a kimona. The blurb at the top of the book reads, "The haunting novel of love in Shangri-La." The back cover indicates "over 2,000,000 copies in print." the typeset is also noticibly different from the first printing.

Another interesting printing is the 47th which made use of the silver spine which Pocket Books adopted in 1952. Beginning with this 1961 printing, LOST HORIZON saw not only a cover change but also a number change and price change. This printing even has a statement indicating these changes. It reads:

In June, 1939, it became the first title in

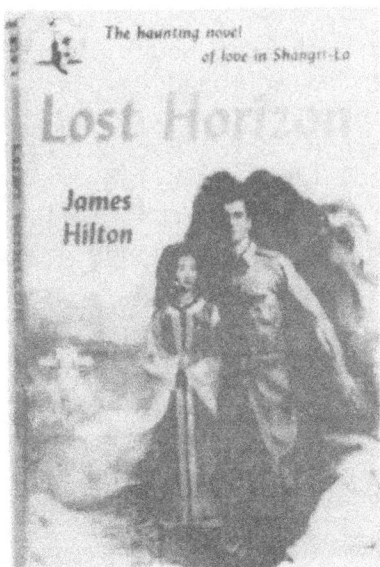

Tom Dunn

Pocket Book #1, 43rd printing, 1959

Pocket Book #6100, 47th printing, 1961

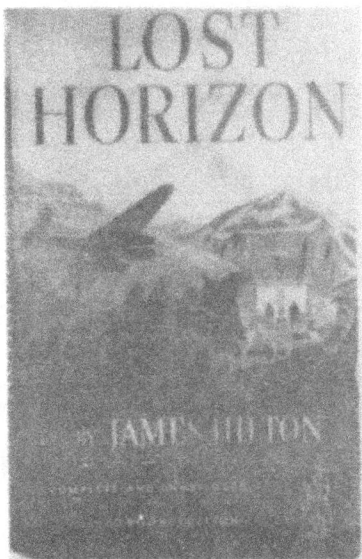

Steinberg

Pocket Book #1, 34th printing, 1945

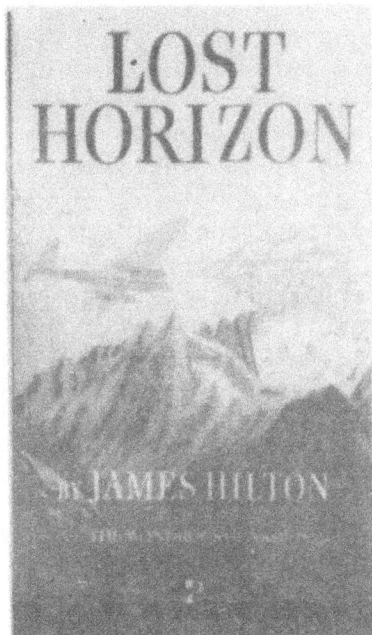

Terry McKee

Pocket Book #83201-8, 80th printing, 1979

the first list published by Pocket Books, Inc.,
the firm which began the "paper-bound revolution" in modern publishing. For twenty-one
and a half years it remained Pocket Book #1 at
25¢, through forty-six printings totaling
nearly 2,000,000 copies. Finally, in 1961 it,
too, yielded to the increase in prices and
became POCKET BOOK #6100 at 35¢.

It's interesting to note that the 47th printing
boasts 'nearly 2,000,000 copies' in print whereas
the 43rd printing boasts that number as well.
And though there are numerous changes, there are
also several carry-overs from the 43rd printing.
Both the 43rd and 47th printings use the same
front cover blurb already mentioned. And though
the back covers have comletely different designs,
they both have the same back-cover blurb. Both
printings also use the same printing plates.
     Of special interest when comparing LOST HORIZON
printings is the 17th printing Pan English edition.
Pan Books first published LOST HORIZON in 1947.
This 1976, 17th printings is a special promotional
edition for the Shangri-La hotel in Singapore. The
back cover even features a drawing of the Shangri-
La hotel and indicates, "with the compliments of
Shangri-La hotel." I wish more hotels would give
paperback books instead of matchbooks as souvenirs.
     The most recent printing of LOST HORIZON is
the 80th Pocket Book printing. This new printing
features a re-drawing by Terry McKee from the
original Steinberg cover of the 1939 edition.
According to Elizabeth Irwin of Pocket Books, they
"would have used the original art except the plates
had been destroyed." There are only slight differ-
ences between the two covers and it's fun to com-
pare the two. Even the back cover of the 80th
printing has the same 3/8th inch canary yellow
border that the first printing has. Oddly enough
Pocket Books makes no mention that they have

resurrected the original cover with the help of a new cover artist. Even the style and size of type used for the title and author's name are very similar on the 1st and 80th printings. At the bottom of the most recent printing are the words: "THE WONDROUS CLASSIC!". Though Pocket Books no doubt is referring to the text, I can't help thinking of the cover.

Pan Book, 17th printing, 1976

■■■■■■■■■■■■■■■■■■■■■■■■■■■■

Bunker Books

M.C. Hill
P.O. Box 1638
Spring Valley, CA 92077

The Plantation Novel:
Paperback Genre of the 1970s?
by Christopher D. Geist

One of the paperback publishing sensations of the 1970s was the enormously successful "plantation" novel. Loosely descended from UNCLE TOM'S CABIN, the works of Thomas Nelson Page, GONE WITH THE WIND, and the bosom and bravado historicals of Frank Yerby, the genre is part of a general resurgence of paperback historical romances. Though there are similarities between plantation novels (alternatively referred to as "slave" novels) and the tumultuous and romantic novels of Rosemary Rogers and her colleagues, the recent plantation books owe their greatest debt to Kyle Onstott's MANDINGO (1957). Yerby's books were among the first to add sex to the portrayal of the antebellum South, but Onstott's remarkably successful volume shifted the focus toward miscegenation and violence.

Every major paperback publishing house has issued works in the genre, though Fawcett is the undeniable champion. Sales figures, while always rather difficult to uncover in the world of mass-market publishing, show that many works have become widely popular. MANDINGO, for example, had sold over four and one-half million copies through July of 1975. Onstott, with the considerable

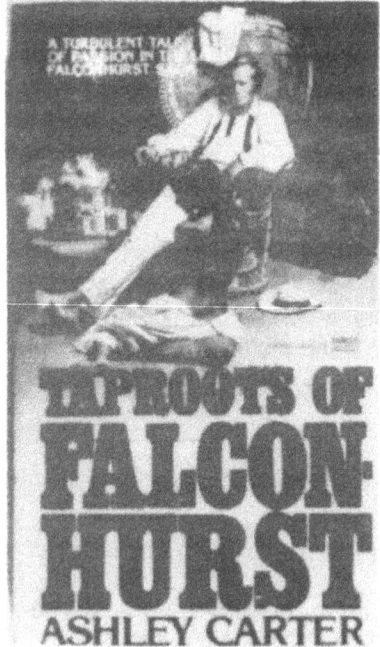

aid of Lance Horner, also
published seven other
novels in the MANDINGO
series. By the close of
the decade sales in the
series were over twenty
million copies. Horner
and Onstott are now dead,
but the series has recently been continued by the
prolific Harry Whittington.
His TAPROOTS OF FALCON-
HURST appeared early in
1979. [1]

Whittington also writes
another series for Fawcett
under the pseudonym of
Ashley Carter. These nov-
els, the Blackoaks saga,
sell over three-quarters
of a million copies each
in a matter of a few

Stan Borack

months. Whittington also edited and rewrote much of a novel left by Lance Horner at the time of his death. This work, THE GOLDEN STUD, was published under Horner's name in 1975, and has since reached one and one-half million readers. Whittington later prepared a sequel, SWORD OF THE GOLDEN STUD (1977), which was issued under the Carter pseudonym.[2]

Novels in the genre generally follow the rise and fortunes of a single plantation, the white family which owns it, and slaves who work it over a lengthy period of time. Such a narrative structure leads naturally to sequels, and authors tend to close one novel in a sufficiently open-ended manner to draw readers back for another installment. If the first work is successful, the publishing house will ask the author to continue the series. Norman Daniels, who has had success in many popular genres, published LAW OF THE LASH in 1968 and its sequel, MASTER OF WYNDWARD, in 1969. Both sold well, but both were rather short. Lancer, the publisher, went bankrupt, and the books were reissued by Warner Books as a lengthy, one-volume novel entitled WYNDWARD PASSION (1978). Within two months of the reissue (initial print run of 400,000) Daniels was asked to continue the saga of Wyndward plantation through five more novels.[3]

There were several other series doing quite well through the end of 1979. The Sabrehill novels by Raymond Giles, the Windhaven Series by Marie de Jourlet, and the Bondmaster books of Richard Tresill-ian are among the most successful. Except for the Tresillian products, each of these series takes its title from the plantation around which the narrative centers. Presumably, contented readers return as each installment becomes available. One fan wrote Richard Tresillian and asked,

Can you tell me, are you planning more of these books[the bondmaster series]? What I am getting at is I am wondering if you are going to follow the pattern of the authors Lance Horner and Kyle On-stott who wrote the Falconhurst series? I would certainly hope so, so that I could collect your complete works as they are published as I did theirs

Readers who join the series in midstream may be
counted on to purchase earlier installments. In an
effort to maintain reader interest, the publishers
of the first number in the Windhaven saga included
a sneak preview chapter from the second novel. The
sequel approach must certainly work, or the publishers would discontinue its use.[4]

Several other important paperback authors have
penned plantation/slave novels. Eric Corder has
contributed SLAVE (1967), THE LONG TATTO (1968),
SLAVE SHIP (1969), HELLBOTTOM (1972), and SAVAGE
RITE (1976). Though the novels are only partially
related, Corder's publisher, Pocket Books, collected
all five together in a volume entitled SHAME AND
GLORY in 1978. Julie Ellis's popular plantation
novels include EDEN, written in 1976, and THE
MAGNOLIAS, which was issued the following year.
Frank Schaefer and Kerry Newcomb, writing as Peter
Gentry, have given us RAFE (1976) and TITUS GAMBLE
(1977). W.E. Dan Ross, who has authored hundreds
of paperback originals in numerous genres, wrote
DELTA FLAME (1978) and several others under his
Marilyn Ross pseudonym.

These novels are
set most often in one of
the slaveholding states
of the American South
(sometimes on a Caribbean
island) during the time
from 1820 to 1860. The
action takes place around
a major plantation, usu-
ally far larger and more
wealthy than was typical
of the antebellum South
historians have come to
know. Though other
crops are raised, it
quickly becomes apparent
that young slaves sired
by the "plantation stud,"
an exotic African with

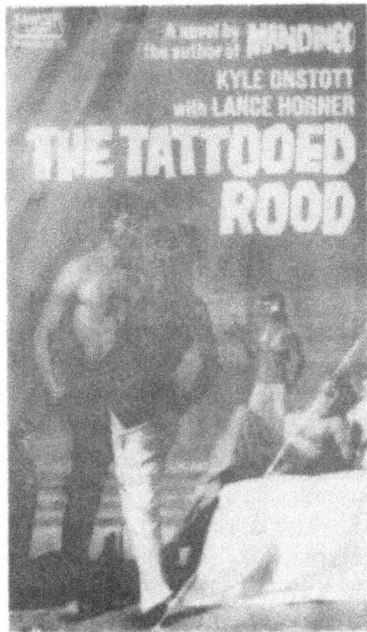

an unusual name and enor-
mous genitals, are the
most important cash crop.
This slave has complete
"wenching privileges,"
and his major task is
to impregnate the doz-
ens of young and beau-
tiful "breeding wench-
es" the master has
assembled for that
purpose.

A LANCE HORNER NOVEL

SECRET OF
BLACKOAKS
BY ASHLEY CARTER

The white master
is often a despicable
character, given to
drink and lusting after
the young female slaves.
He frequently has a beau-
tiful white wife, but he
clearly prefers to take sexual advantage of the
slave girls. The wife, disconsolate because her
husband has rejected her, looks for sex outside her
marriage and winds up in bed with the slave stud.
Her husband discovers the liason, is horrified at
the miscegenation, and violently punishes the er-
rant lovers. For example, MANDINGO concludes as
the wife is poisoned and her black lover is boiled
alive. The slave lover of THE BONDMASTER'S wife is
barbecued alive. She is forced to eat his flesh
and is finally shoved to her death in the barbecue
pit beside the slave.

Though some variation of this scenario provides the dramatic focus in numerous plantation
novels, several other patterns of action are also
popular. Slave uprisings and rebellions are frequently a major part of these tales, as in Newcomb
and Schaefer's RAFE, Corder's SLAVE SHIP, and
Norman Daniels' SLAVE REBELLION (1970). Renegade
slaves form a sort of terrorist organization in the
Sabrehill books of Raymond Giles (SABREHILL, 1974;
SLAVES OF SABREHILL, 1975; and REBELS OF SABREHILL,
1976). This series also examines the difficulties

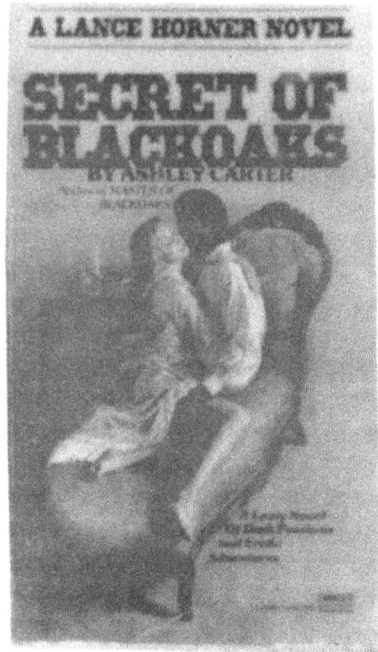

of a white woman who has inherited a plantation.
Although Lucy Sabre is a fine manager, she must
constantly face the disapproval of sexism of the
neighboring white males who believe that it is sin-
ful and dangerous for a young, beautiful white
woman to live and work so closely to male slaves.
There is no white man on the Sabrehill plantation.

Another significant theme explores the rise
and fall of the antebellum slave society. Here,
the novelists trace the development of a plantation
from its earliest beginnings, through a high point
of wealth and style in the early 1850s, to its final
destruction just prior to or during the Civil War.
In RAFE a bloody slave revolt brings on the estate's
demise, while the planter's mismanagement, sexual
depravity, and greed lead to the decline of Harry
Whittington's BLACKOAKS plantation. The Civil War
is responsible in CHINABERRY, an excellent plantation novel written by William Lavender in 1976.
This pattern seems to be developing in Daniels'
Wyndward books. One author, Morris Hershman, believes that this "rise and fall" scenario provides
an important appeal to plantation literature. "The
South and its plantation owners," he says, "are as
close as America has ever come to a native aristocracy; and in this kind of book the aristocracy is
destroyed. Audiences like to read about the rich
and mighty being humbled, I think."[5]

But there are other reasons for the marketa-
bility of plantation/slave novels. Since most of
the novels deal in various forms of interracial
sexuality, it seems possible that readers enjoy
the genre for its exploration of this traditional
taboo. Thus, the novelists provide the audience,
especially white males, with fantasies of tasting
forbidden fruit. "Fantasies is right," suggests
Norman Daniels. "We use whatever becomes part of
the novel, but white male and black female seems
the most prevalent. Though the opposite is also
used to a certain extent. Whatever makes the novel
more interesting and supplies a sex tease." Morris
Hershman concurs, "When you write about fantasies

of interracial sex as imagined by white readers, you're probably on safe ground." But Richard Tresillian objects, "The popularity of my own books with both blacks and whites has always intrigued me and makes me think that the appeal of white sexual fantasies...is not the complete reason for the genre's success."[6]

Tresillian goes on to assert, "The readability of the story...should not be overlooked." He is undoubtedly correct. The genre's possibilities for adventure and intrigue are limited only by the skills of the writers.

"My partner [Kerry Newcomb] and I write stories, tell tales," writes Frank Schafer. "We have no presumptions to artistic merit when it comes to genre books. We try to tell a good yarn more than anything else." And the team *does* spin good yarns, as anyone who has read RAFE will attest. The authors' talent is all the more impressive when the novel's plot is scrutinized. It is really a fairly basic story, but the manner in which it is dramatized renders it successful. This talent factor partially accounts for the fact that a few authors sell far more books than most in the overcrowded world of plantation fiction.[7]

Norman Daniels believes that these novels received an important boost from the unprecedented popularity of Alex Haley's ROOTS, both the book and television series. This certainly accounts for many of the plantation novels issued during the summer of 1977, shortly after ROOTS became television's all-time ratings champion. But, as most commercial authors realize, genres come and go, and the market for plantation novels may currently be on the downswing, at least for a time. "While I hope this popularity continues," Harry Whittington says, "the very weight of novels may tear it down." Schaefer and Newcomb have already backed away from the genre. Schaefer notes, "I think the general reading public goes from genre to genre, wears one out and seeks something new. After a while passes, there is a new audience, and the cycle starts again."

Dan Ross believes there are other reasons for the
apparent decline of this literature: "I'm reason-
ably sure the publishers with their demands for
soft pornography in historical romances are going
to eventually kill the credibility of the genre.
This is sad, for it could be a respectable medium."
Perhaps we will not see many plantation novels in
the 1980s--but they *will* be back.[8]

NOTES

[1]Earl Bargainnier, "The Falconhurst Series: A
New Popular Image of the Old South," JOURNAL OF POP-
ULAR CULTURE, X (Fall, 1976), 298-314, and letter
from Harry Whittington to Christopher Geist, June
29, 1978.
    [2]Letter from Harry Whittington to Christopher
Geist, June 7, 1978.
    [3]Letter from Norman Daniels to Christopher
Geist, May 15, 1978.
    [4]Letter from Hal Hawkey to Richard Tresillian,
April 28, 1978. Mr. Tresillian was kind enough to
furnish a photocopy of the letter. The sneak pre-
view appears in Marie de Jourlet, WINDHAVEN PLANTA-
TION, Pinnacle Books, 1977. The other books in this
series include STORM OVER WINDHAVEN, 1977, and
LEGACY OF WINDHAVEN, 1978, both published by Pin-
nacle. Lyle Kenyon Engle, who "produced" John Jakes'
Bicentennial Series, also is listed as "producer"
of the Windhaven books.
    [5]Letter from Morris Hershman to Christopher
Geist, May 6, 1978.
    [6]I explore the sexual appeal of these novels
in detail in "Violence, Passion, and Sexual Racism:
The Plantation Novel in the 1970s," SOUTHERN QUAR-
TERLY, forthcoming issue. Daniels to Geist, May 15,
1978; Hershman to Geist, May 6, 1978; and Tresillian
to Geist, May 24, 1978.
    [7]Ibid.; letter from Frank Schaefer to Geist,
May 12, 1978.
    [8]Daniels to Geist, May 15, 1978; Harry Whitting-
ton to Geist, March 1, 1978; Schaefer to Geist, May
12, 1978; and W.E. Dan Ross to Geist, May 10, 1978.
49

Book Sellers

The following people sell paperbacks. Most mail out booklists on a regular basis and all are knowledgeable paperback collectors.

BILL & PAT LYLES
77 High Street
Greenfield, MA 01301
(413) 774-2432

VIVA BOOKS
365 E. Cuyahoga Falls Ave.
Akron, OH 44310

SCOTT OWEN
P.O. Box 343
Moraga, CA 94556

GRAVESEND BOOKS
Box 235
Poconopines, PA 18350
(717) 646-3317

THE LEFT HAND OF DARKNESS
Jan Landau
441 Ford St. #8
West Conshohocken, PA 19428

JUDY K. REYNOLDS
9969 B Sloanes Sq.
St. Louis, MO 63134
(314) 429-6654

JEFF MEYERSON
50 First Place
Brooklyn, N.Y. 11231

JACK IRWIN
16 Gloucester Lane
Trenton, N.J. 08618

MICHAEL BARSON
3216 Martha Custis Dr.
Alexandria, VA 22302
(703) 998-8284

BILL LIPPINCOTT
Dunbar Hill Rd.
North Anson, ME 04958

ED KALB
3227 E. Enid Ave.
Mesa, Arizona 85204
(602) 830-1855

JEFF PATTON
3621 Carolina St., N.W.
Massillon, OH 44646

STEVE LEWIS
62 Chestnut St.
Newington, CT 06111

Mc CLINTOCK BOOKS
P.O. Box 3111
Warren, OH 44485
(216) 399-7348

JOAN WATERHOUSE
P.O. Box 167
West Upton, MA 01587
(617) 529-3703

BUNKER BOOKS
P.O. Box 1638
Spring Valley, CA 92077
(714) 469-3296

PAPERBACK PARADISE
468 Centre St.
Jamaica Plain, MA 02130

BARRY & WALLY PATTENGILL
Rt. 3 Box 508
Waco, Texas 76708

THE OLD BOOK STORE
210 E. Cuyahoga Falls Ave.
Akron, Ohio 44310
(216) 253-5025

MURDER BY THE BOOK
194½ Atwells Ave.
Providence, RI 02903

If you are a bookseller and would like your name and address printed in "Book Sellers," please drop us a line. Please tell us if you sell paperbacks by mail and/or have a retail store. We are also interested if you mail out lists on a regular basis. Happy Paperback Hunting!

The Mike Shayne Caper
by Bernard A. Drew

In a good Mike Shayne detective thriller, just as you're approaching the climax and think you have things figured out--pow! There's a surprise ending.

It works the same way with the writer. Just when you're sure Davis Dresser has been hiding behind the Brett Halliday pseudonym all these years, Robert Terrall of Cornwall, Connecticut, admits that he's been ghostwriting the books since the mid 1950s.

Terrall, animated speaker and engaging storyteller, explained his craft and relationship with the popular fictional detective, Shayne, at a talk at the Cornwall Library recently.

"Dave Dresser originated the Shayne books. He always wanted to be a writer, but he never was a very good one," said Terrall.

After submitting manuscripts for a few years, he finally in 1939 found a home for his hard-

Photo Courtesy Bernard Drew

Robert Terrall

51

Robert McGinnis

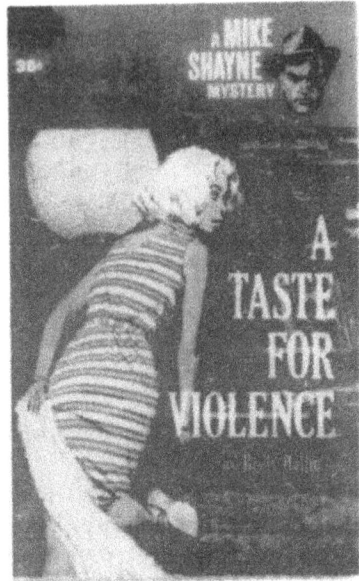

Robert McGinnis

boiled detective. The critics weren't overly
enthusiastic about the hero, according to Terrall's
telling, but the motion picture industry within a
short time latched onto him for a series of low-
budget movies starring Lloyd Nolan.

"Originally, Shayne had a wife, Phyllis, as a
nod to Dashiell Hammett's popular Thin Man," said
Terrall. "It was a husband and wife comedy. But
Shayne's wife, Phyllis, was terrible. She was al-
ways wrinkling her nose or stamping her tiny foot.
She died inexplicably between books."

"Actually, the economics of the film deal
killed her. Dresser sold the character for $1000,
and every time they made a new picture they would
pay him $1000. If they used one of his book plots,
they would pay more. When the movie studio said it
couldn't use the team idea, he went home and killed
her off. The books were picked up immediately after
that," he said.

With the paperback explosion of the 1950s,

52

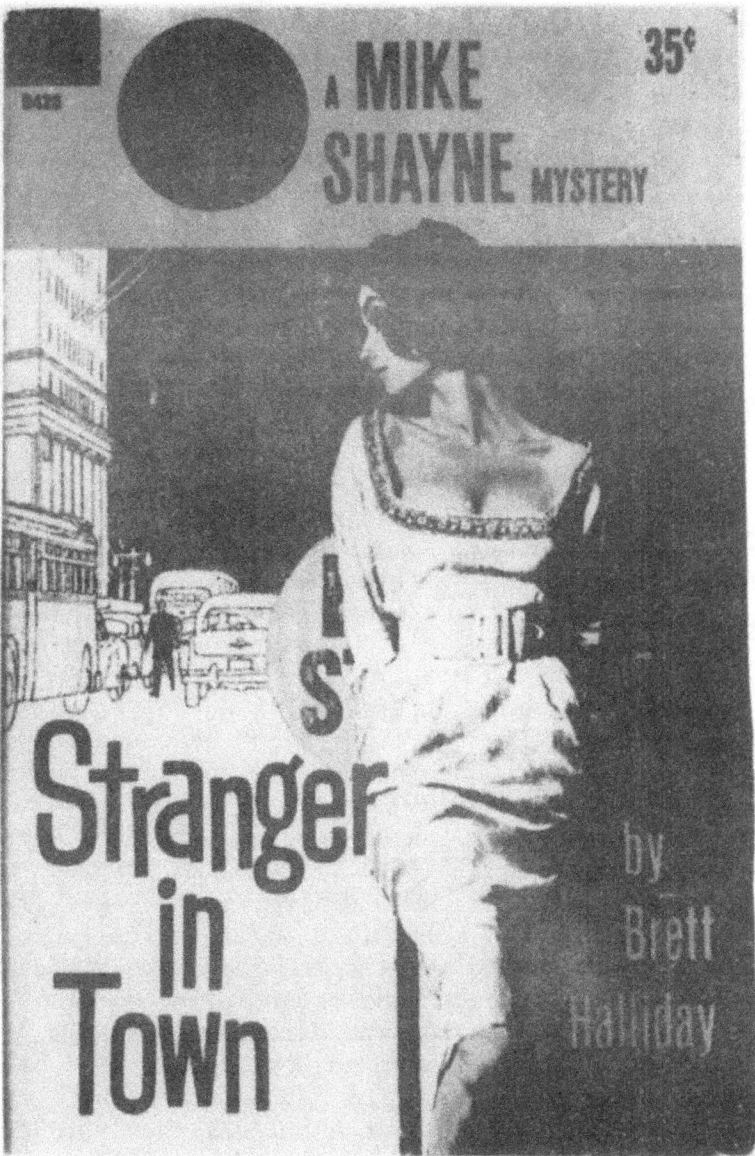

A MIKE SHAYNE MYSTERY

35¢

D428

Stranger in Town

by Brett Halliday

Shayne found a mass audience and became a staple of the Dell line. But Dresser developed a writer's block, according to Terrall. The series editors, not wanting to abandon a good thing, engaged new writers to continue the Shayne saga under the Brett Halliday by-line. Terrall was the last of the new writers.

"At the time, I was attempting to write commercial fiction for four months of the year," he said, "and good stuff the other eight months. I had two series myself then, at Dell and Fawcett (under pseudonyms)."

As he undertook the new assignment, Terrall made a careful study of the character.

"In the world of fiction, there are two types of heroes," he said. "There are the strong, valiant Achilles and the wily, crafty Odysseus. It was a problem for mystery fiction writers to choose between them. Some used two characters, such as Rex Stout's Nero Wolfe and Archie Goodwin. Others fudged the issue. Sherlock Holmes, for example, often turns into an athlete in the last chapter. Where he got the muscles, nobody knows. Brain suddenly turns to brawn."

Terrall saw that Dresser tried to incorporate both qualities in one figure, and he found the attributes that made Shayne such an appealing hero to a wide readership.

"I noted that Shayne never won a fight," he said. "But he was frequently knocked down by hoodlums. I think the ordinary reader liked to feel he could win a fight, but realistically knew he would end up on the floor. Shayne was described in one way--as tough--and depicted in another."

Similarly, Shayne was said to be irresistible to women, yet he never much more than kissed his literary girlfriends. The red-headed private eye drank cognac by the gallon, but never got drunk. And, though he earned huge fees, he still lived in the same, seedy Miami apartment.

Terrall incorporated these ingredients and others in his successful pastiches. Typically, in

54

MURDER SPINS THE WHEEL, we read:

> Shayne grabbed upward through the
> blur and dazzle. His fingers closed on
> the big man's shirt and dragged him down.
> He had no leverage, and for the moment
> there was no strength in his arms. He
> twisted his knuckles in the big man's
> eye, to mark him so he would know him
> if he ever saw him again....Three of
> them, the redhead noted, and another
> small explosion went off inside his
> skull. His grip on the big man's shirt
> front loosened. He was kicked twice more,
> and then they left him.

The series took on new life with its new
ghost-writer. It thrived through the early 1970s,
when a blunder in cover designs and the explosion
on the paperback racks of mafia-killing, executioner-
type thrillers diminished sales.

"When the series began to go soft," said the
writer, "the publisher decided to bring it into the
world with photograph covers. The art director at
the time was homosexual, and the model he hired was
a friend of his.

"The model was small, and he was photographed
from an angle so that the women in the pictures would
not tower over him."

"He didn't look like the redhead readers had
come to know."

Terrall suggested bluntly that the model's
appearance helped accelerate Shayne's decline.
The publisher pulled the poor-selling covers, and
put out ones featuring photos of women only, but
the damage had been done.

Dresser, who was still earning an income from
his character--the sixty some-odd titles sold in
the vicinity of sixty to seventy-five million copies
--died in 1977, in destitution, said Terrall.

The Connecticut author didn't mind seeing the
Shayne series end. "Writing the Shaynes was getting

more difficult," he said. "I was doing a better job and it was taking longer to finish them."

Under his own name, Terrall has recently published THE SAND DOLLAR and LUCK BE A LADY.

Northwoods Funnies

Bill Lippincott
Dunbar Hill Road ● No Anson, ME 04958

CURRENT LIST: "Mystery, Adventure and Fantasy" hardcovers (with a sprinkling of paperbacks) 50 cents plus SASE Biggers, Carr, Christie, Hammett, Hume, Queen, Rice, Wallace, Woolrich, Brand, Chambers, Curwood, Doyle, Friel, Grey, Lamb, London, Sabatini, Rohmer, Baum, Burgess, Cabell, Dunsany, Howard, Morris....special section of pulp writers....illustrators....etc.

COMING IN JUNE: "Paperbacks: Spring 1980" send $1.00 before June 1st.

■■■■■■■■■■■■■■■■■■■■■■■■■■■■■

CHECKLISTS

AVAILABLE IN ONE BOUND VOLUME

Ace (1-411)
Dell (1-1590)
Pocket Books (1-500)
Popular Library (1-835)
Armed Services Editions (1-1322)
Avon (1-864)

Available from M.C. Hill, Bunker Books, P.O. Box 1638 Spring Valley, CA 92077. The price is $6.75 plus 75 cents for postage and handling.